How to teach this unit

The UK is a maritime nation, with nowhere more than 60 miles from the sea, so it is self-evident that children should develop some knowledge and understanding about the environment where land and sea interact. Coasts provide a particularly appropriate context for exploring and investigating key geographical ideas and concepts, such as physical processes and human effects on the environment; physical changes can occur almost every day through the action of the tides. Thanks to seaside holidays and day trips, most children will have a shared understanding of the coast and its features, while those who are fortunate enough to live on or near the coast will be even more familiar with its character.

What do I need to know?

The coast is an environment where physical processes have a clear impact on human activities, and knowledge of these processes is a necessary prerequisite if you are to teach this unit confidently. The processes are not difficult to comprehend, however, and much rests on an understanding of waves, tides and their impact on different types of coastal features.

The CD-Rom contains further information about the physical processes and human features that occur on coasts.

Waves and erosion

Waves are usually created by the action of the wind on the surface of the sea – the exceptions are **tsunamis**, which are the result of undersea earth movements. When waves reach the shore they can be either destructive or constructive. **Destructive waves** are high and have a great deal of energy. **Constructive waves** have less energy, and the action of the **swash** (a wonderful onomatopoeic word) can move material up a beach.

Waves **erode** softer rock on the coast into bays, leaving headlands of harder rock protruding into the sea. Erosion is at its greatest where large waves break against a cliff. Slowly the waves undercut the foot of the cliff, and over time it is undermined and collapses. As this process is repeated, the cliff will retreat, leaving an expanse of gently sloping rock at its foot. This area will be covered at high tide and exposed when the tide is out – it is the site of the rock pools that children love to explore on a rocky shore.

On headlands where resistant rocks have cracks and faults, erosion will widen any weakness to form, initially, a **cave**. If the headland is relatively narrow, eventually wave action will cut through to form a natural **arch**. As the waves continue to erode, sooner or later the roof of the arch will collapse, leaving an isolated **stack**. See illustration on CD; these could also make a simple sequencing activity for less able pupils.

Because waves rarely approach a beach at right angles, they cause movement of material along the shore – **longshore drift**. Wooden barriers called **groynes** are built to slow down the movement.

Tides

The tide is the regular rising and falling of the sea's surface caused by changes in gravitational forces. At any point on the coast, there are normally two high tides and two low tides each day.

Human features

It is possible to categorise places on the coast by the types of human features which are evident there. In places such as river mouths and deep-water bays, fishing and trading ports have grown. In places with attractive beaches, tourist resorts have developed. Coastlines distant from population centres and/or unsuitable for ports have remained largely unspoilt. Such coasts still suffer from tourism pressures, however, and some have attracted attention as potential locations for wind farms.

Human features can contribute to erosion on the coast. Buildings on cliff tops can increase the instability of cliffs, resulting in landslips. Concrete sea walls are built at the base of cliffs, and **gabions** (huge metal baskets filed with stones and boulders) are placed to reinforce coasts threatened by erosion.

Misconceptions

Two obvious misconceptions may become apparent when children are investigating coasts:

You may find that they do not understand the difference between **waves** and **tides**. It is important to emphasise that, although the waves appear to roll in and out constantly on a beach, the sea as a whole moves in and out from the shore twice a day by a much greater amount.

Another misconception may arise from the use of simulations and diagrams of coastal processes – children may assume that these processes happen over a very short timescale. It is important to emphasise and re-emphasise that these are long-term processes.

Vocabulary

In his summary of research into the acquisition of geographical vocabulary in *Primary Sources: Research Findings in Primary Geography* (Scoffham, 1998), Ward points out that children's understanding of some taken-for-granted geographical terms may be imperfect, even at Year 6. He quotes research which found that words like 'cliff' and 'erosion' were only correctly defined by 30% of 11-year-old children. He also notes that some coast-related words are confusing because they are homonyms or homophonic words – 'beach', 'drift' and 'shore' are examples. It may help to clarify these terms by using good-quality visual images.

Where do I start?

Starting points

Because most children will have a degree of familiarity with coastal environments, it is important to use their personal experience as a starting point for lessons and tasks. Images and maps can be used as prompts for recalling physical and human features observed at seaside locations. The clarification and use of key geographical terms will also be important. Getting the children to make concept or 'mind' maps of coast-related terms will be a useful precursor to the unit, as will a similar exercise at the end for assessment purposes. Do the children show a greater understanding of these terms at the end than at the start?

ICT skills

As the unit is aimed at upper key stage 2 pupils, the ICT skills involved should be within their capabilities. However, before carrying out Task 3, it would be useful to give them some experience of UK-based mapping tools on the Internet, such as www.multimap.com or www.mapquest.com. This task also demands some familiarity with the conventions of oblique aerial photographs.

The unit contains four lessons with significant ICT elements. One of these requires the use of an interactive whiteboard or large screen for whole-class teaching (Task 2); the others require networked computers and an Internet connection. Management of these tasks will depend very much on the availability of resources in your school – in a high-resource setting such as an ICT suite, they could be carried out as class lessons, with introduction, group tasks and plenary taking place in one session. In a setting with fewer resources (e.g. one or two networked computers in a classroom), the introduction and plenary can be undertaken with the whole class, but the tasks will have to be carried out over a longer timescale, with groups visiting workstations on a rota or similar basis.

Conservation

Some exploration of the idea of conservation will be useful before Tasks 5 and 6 are attempted. There may be a building or physical feature in or near the school locality that is protected from development, and children could to be asked to consider why this is so. Or they could be presented with the proposition that a favourite place known to them (e.g. a playground or park) is to be changed and/or developed – how would they feel? Either or both of these tasks might give the children some insight into why 'Heritage Coasts' are protected, and the strong feelings that are engendered when landscapes are threatened by development.

Time allocation

The teaching time available for geography can vary enormously. SuperSchemes units have been written with three possibilities in mind:

- a **short-medium** unit *(5-10 hours)*
- a **long** unit *(10-15 hours)*
- a **continuous** unit *(15-30 minutes per week)*

The medium term plans allow you to choose an appropriate length for your particular class. Some of the longer medium term plans offer enough material for you to continue with the topic later in the year.

Key questions

The tasks set in the **Medium Term Plan** address the following key questions:

Task 1

- What is a coast?

- What physical (natural) and human features would you expect to find on the coast?

- Can you identify these features in images and on maps?

The questions are explored through tasks which will develop children's graphicacy skills through the use of images and maps.

Task 2

- How does the tide affect the appearance of the coast?

The task here is to predict the appearance of a coast at high and low tides, bearing in mind the physical features that are present.

Task 3

- What geographical processes occur on a coast?

- Can you identify signs of erosion and deposition on a coast?

The main task here is to identify characteristic signs of erosion and deposition in visual images (low-level, oblique aerial photographs) of a distant location.

Task 4

- How do the processes of erosion, deposition and drift work?

This task involves the use of a computer simulation to show the action of coastal processes over a greatly shortened timescale.

Task 5

- Why should some coasts be protected?

The main task involves a structured enquiry using a website, with a possible extension into wider internet searching for specific information. To complete the task, children will select, combine and interpret information from a source.

Task 6

- What are the cases for and against the building of wind turbines in coastal locations, either on or offshore?

The children are asked to explore a highly relevant and contemporary issue from the point of view of proponents and opponents: renewable energy and its impact on the environment.

Task 7

- What is your favourite place on the coast?

- Why?

The task here focuses on a creative response to a coastal environment and the expression of ideas and preferences through artwork.

Concept map

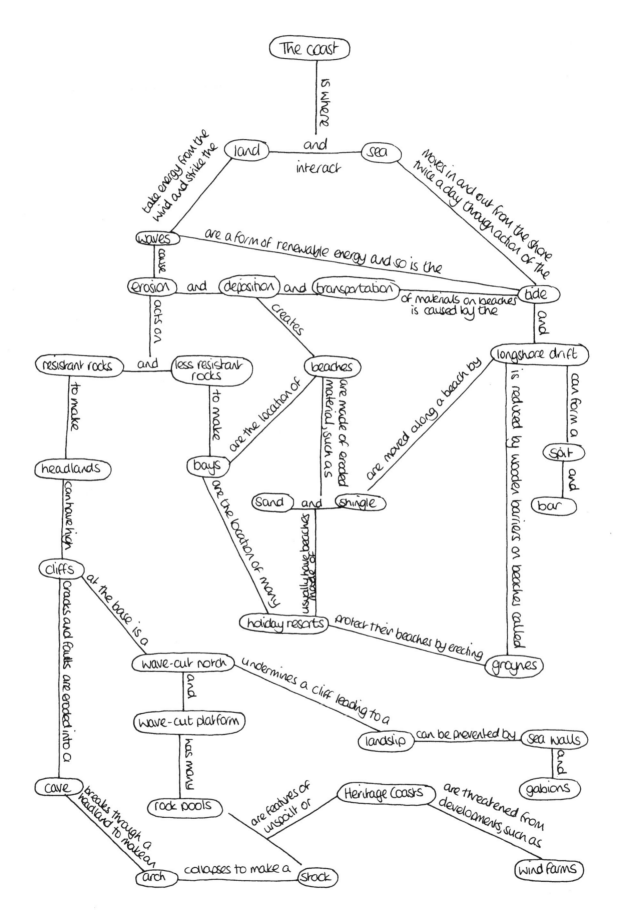

The coast

is where

land and sea interact

take energy from the wind and strike the

Moves in and out from the shore twice a day through action of the

waves are a form of renewable energy and so is the tide

cause

erosion and deposition and transportation of materials on beaches is caused by the

acts on

creates

and

longshore drift

resistant rocks and less resistant rocks

are the location of

beaches are made of eroded material such as

are moved along a beach by

is reduced by wooden barriers on beaches called

can form a

to make

to make

spit and bar

headlands

bays

Sand and shingle

can have high

are the location of many

usually have beaches made of

Cliffs

Cracks and faults are eroded into a

at the base is a

holiday resorts protect their beaches by erecting groynes

wave-cut notch

undermines a cliff leading to a

and

wave-cut platform

has many

landslip can be prevented by sea walls

and

cave

breaks through a headland to make an

rock pools

are features of unspoilt or

Heritage Coasts are threatened from developments such as

gabions

arch collapses to make a stack

wind farms

Medium term plan: Investigating coasts (using maps and images)

Learning outcomes	Key questions	Pupil activities	Resources/ key vocabulary	Assessment opportunities
To show knowledge and understanding of the characteristic human and physical features of coastal environments.	What is a coast? What human features would you expect to find on the coast? What physical (natural) features would you expect to find on the coast? Can you identify these features on an OS map?	**Task 1** Ask the children what the term 'coast' means to them. List the children's ideas. Provide images of different coasts around the UK. In small groups, children use the images to identify human and physical features found on coasts. Move around the groups and introduce terms to describe the features, when appropriate, e.g. beach, cliff, bay, headland, sea wall, groyne, gabion, etc. Ask the children to identify different types of coasts in the images, e.g. wild (undeveloped) coasts, tourist coasts, urban (built-up) coasts, changing coasts. Provide the groups with OS map extracts showing different types of coasts. Sort these coasts using the same categories. Ask children to list the typical features of a particular type of coast using both maps and images, e.g. hotels, sandy beaches, crowds on a tourist coast. Revisit the children's ideas from the first activity. Do they want to change their list of what the term 'coast' means to them? **Activity sheet 1 may act as a revision sheet for the activities covered in this lesson.**	Images of coasts around the UK (appropriate images can be found on a range of websites – see **Resources** section on CD-Rom). OS map extracts at 1:25 000 and 1:50 000 scales showing a range of coasts (download and print from www.ordnancesurvey.co.uk/ oswebsite/getamap). *Coast, human features, physical features, undeveloped, tourist, beach, cliff, headland, bay, sea wall, groyne, gabion, wave cut platform.*	Can a pupil recognise human and physical features characteristic of coasts? Can a pupil identify human and physical features of coasts as represented on OS maps? Can a pupil identify and describe different types of coast?
To show understanding of the effects of daily changes in coastal environments.	What changes occur on coasts every day? What is the coast like at high tide? What is the coast like at low tide?	**Task 2 See Example Lesson Plan** Ask the children if they have seen the coast at different times of day? Have they seen any changes? Talk about the tide and how it covers and reveals the shoreline twice a day. Show the image of part of the shore at Flamborough Head in North Yorkshire. Point out the features: cliffs, cave, stack, wave-cut rock platform, etc. Explain that the picture shows a time between low and high tide. Ask the children to make annotated sketches, labelling the features, to show how the scene might appear (a) at low tide and (b) at high tide. **See Activity sheet 2.** Discuss with the children what might be revealed when the tide is fully out, e.g. a rocky beach, shingle. Also discuss the habitats in the image, and what plants and animals live in the tidal zone. Share children's sketches and ideas in a plenary – focus, particularly, on their ideas about what might be revealed at low tide.	Flamborough Head photograph. *Cave, stack, cliff, wave-cut rock platform, beach, tide, tidal zone.*	Can a pupil identify the features in the photograph? Can a pupil relate the features to the processes shown in the simulation? Can a pupil predict the appearance of the coast at high and low tide? Can a pupil justify his/her inclusion of specific features in an annotated sketch?

Medium term plan:
Investigating coasts (using ICT resources)

Learning outcomes	Key questions	Pupil activities	Resources/ key vocabulary	Assessment opportunities
To show knowledge and understanding of coastal processes, e.g. erosion, deposition, drift.	What geographical processes occur on the coast? Can you identify the results of wave action on the coast? Can you identify places where the coast is being eroded? Can you identify places where the coast is being built up?	**Task 3** Explain to the children that the coast is the place where land and sea interact. It is constantly changing, over short and long timescales. Explain that in the previous lesson we looked at coastal locations around the UK, but in this lesson we are going to look at the coastline in a distant place – California in the USA. Point out that, despite its distant location, the California coast is subject to the same processes as in the UK. Find California on a world map. Discuss with the children the distance, the direction and their predictions as to its appearance. Identify any places in California known to the children. Discuss with the children any evidence they might look for in pictures indicating that the coast is being eroded (caves, landslips, lack of beaches) or being built up (wide beaches, sheltered bays, spits). Also discuss ways in which the coast is protected to prevent change (sea walls, etc.). Using a website, ask the children to work in small groups, finding images of different parts of the coast with evidence of erosion, deposition and human action. The images are to be saved to computer for on-screen viewing or printing. In a plenary, groups report back and justify their choices based on evidence in the pictures.	The website at www.californiacoastline.org contains low-level aerial photographs of the California coastline, almost continuously, from Oregon in the north to Mexico in the south. Images can be found by hyperlinks from maps or by other search methods. Changes can be observed by comparing images from 1972 with those from today. *Erosion, deposition, beach, spit, landslip, bay, California.*	Can a pupil identify features of erosion, deposition and human action from aerial photographs? Can they justify their choices of photographs based on visual evidence?
To show knowledge and understanding of how coastal processes change the coastline.	Can you identify the processes that will be at work in this simulation? Can you predict what will happen to features in the simulation as coastal processes occur – the river mouth, the beach, the building on the cliff top?	**Task 4** Explain to the children that, having identified erosional and depositional landforms (e.g. landslips and beaches) using images, we are now going to use a simulation to see how these processes occur. Show the initial screen of the simulation and ask children to predict what will happen in different parts of the scene as time passes and wave action takes effect. In particular, note the river mouth, beach, cliff and cliff-top building. Emphasise that the simulation shows processes working at greatly increased speed. What takes a few seconds on-screen would take many years to happen in the real world. Run the simulation and, at the end, ask children to describe the effects they have seen. Run it again, asking different groups to focus on specific features. Show labels for the processes and use the linked pictures/animations to explain erosion (e.g. cave > arch > stack), deposition and drift in more detail. Ask the children to write diary accounts describing parts of the scene, with yearly (or more widely spaced) entries focusing on the changes that an observer would see on the beach, cliff-top, by the river, etc. The children share their diary entries in a plenary.	Windows PC linked to an interactive whiteboard or large screen. Software: RM Easiteach Geography Content Pack – Investigating Coasts: 'Formation of Coastal Features' simulation. The Institute of Education in London has an Earth Science Centre with hands-on simulation models for exploring coastal processes. *Erosion, deposition, beach, drift, cave, arch, stack, cliff, river, delta.*	Can a pupil predict the effects of coastal processes, based on their prior knowledge after viewing photographs? Can a pupil describe the effects of coastal process in a particular location? Can a pupil distinguish between, erosion, deposition and drift? Can a pupil describe the process of cliff erosion that results in caves, arches and stacks?

Medium term plan:
Investigating coasts (using the internet)

Learning outcomes	Key questions	Pupil activities	Resources/ key vocabulary	Assessment opportunities
To show understanding of reasons why some coasts are protected from development.	Why should some coasts be protected? In what ways are protected coasts threatened?	**Task 5** Remind the children of the images of the unspoilt coasts in Task 1. Explain that coastlines such as these are designated as Heritage Coasts in England and Wales, and are usually protected from development. Ask the children to use the Countryside Agency website (**www.countryside.gov.uk**) to find the nearest Heritage Coast to their locality. Split the children into groups, each with a section of coast, and ask them to use the website to list (a) reasons why the coasts in their section are protected and (b) ways in which they may be under threat. For some sections, further research may be needed, using a child-friendly search engine, e.g. BBCi (www.bbc.co.uk). Ask the groups to summarise their findings on sticky 'post-it' notes. In a plenary, discuss the groups' findings and add the notes to the coastline on a wall map of the British Isles.	Websites: **www.countryside.gov.uk** **www.nationaltrust.org.uk/ coastline** **www.bbc.co.uk.** *Heritage, protection, development, threat.*	Can a pupil identify the nearest Heritage Coast to the school locality? Can a pupil identify a reason why a particular Heritage Coast is protected?
To explain issues relating to development in coastal locations.	What are the cases for and against the building of wind turbines in coastal locations, either on or offshore?	**Task 6** Explain that, because of concern over climate change, the government wants more and more wind farms to be built so that electricity can be produced from renewable energy. Coastal locations (onshore or just offshore) are ideal sites for wind farms. Why? Explain that you are going to split the children up into two groups. The scenario is that one of the Heritage Coasts (or a similar unspoilt coastline in another part of the UK) found in the previous activity has been identified as the best location for large new wind farm to be built either onshore or a short distance offshore. Using a child-friendly search engine, e.g. *BBCi* (**www.bbc.co.uk**), the groups have a limited time to find out the cases for and against wind farms. In a plenary, ask the groups to report back their findings. Emphasise that they must make their case with a particular coastal location in mind.	Website: **www.bbc.co.uk** to search for websites presenting the case for and against coastal wind farms. Useful sites include: **www.bbc.co.uk/climate/ adaptation/wind_power .shtml** British Wind Energy Association **www.bwea.com** National Wind Power **www.natwindpower.co.uk** *Wind farm, turbine, renewable, energy, onshore, offshore.*	Can a pupil identify a reason why unspoilt coastlines should be protected? Can a pupil present a simple but reasoned case for or against coastal wind farms?
To summarise knowledge and understanding about a specific coastal area or location.	What is your favourite place on the coast? Why?	**Task 7 (See also Activity sheet 3)** Britain has a large population for a relatively small island. It has been calculated that, if the population of Great Britain (England, Scotland and Wales) all went to the coast at the same time, each person would have only 3in (8cm) of coast to stand on! Explain to the children that you want them to choose their favourite coastal location – either one they have encountered during the previous activities or one they have visited. Where would their 8cm spot be and why? Ask the children each to identify their favourite coastal place and give three reasons why they like it. The reasons should focus on the features of the place and should be reflected in artwork (e.g. drawing, painting, collage) which clearly shows the place's character. In a plenary, ask the children to share their preferences, their reasons for these, and their artwork.	Resources from previous activities. A choice of materials for drawing, painting and collage, including natural materials such as shells, dried seaweed, etc. *Coast, seashore, features, character.*	Can a pupil express reasons for the choice of a coastal location that focus on its features? Can a pupil reflect the character of a chosen location by visual means?

Lesson plan: What changes occur on coasts every day

Subject: Geography (years 5-6)

Time/Duration: One hour minimum

Learning outcomes

In the lesson children will learn:

- about changes that occur on coasts daily
- to predict the effects of the tide on a specific place
- that the layout of pictures and text on screen or paper can be changed using a simple desktop publishing program
- about the effects of daily changes in coastal environments.

The following questions may be useful for assessment:

Can a pupil:

- identify the features in the photograph? (cave, stack, cliff, wave-cut rock platform, beach, tide, tidal zone)
- relate the features to the processes shown in the simulation?
- predict the appearance of the coast at high and low tide?
- justify the inclusion of specific features in an annotated sketch?

Background to the current lesson

This is the second lesson in the 'Investigating Coasts' unit of work. Previous work will have included identification of human and physical features of the coast in pictures and on maps, and the children will have some ideas about the physical processes that affect coasts and that are responsible for the resulting features.

Lesson details

Introduction

- Ask the children if they have seen the coast at different times of day and what changes they noticed. Talk about the tide, why it occurs, and how it covers and reveals the shoreline twice a day.
- If the children show any confusion in relation to waves and tides, emphasise that, even in high winds, waves roll only a short distance back and forth, while tides change sea levels regularly, by as much as 5 or 6m.
- Show the image of part of the shore at Flamborough Head. Where is this place? Identify its location on a map. What physical features can they see? – cliffs, layers of rock (chalk), cave, stack, wave-cut rock platform, etc. Children may also notice some human features – a path or a marquee.
- Does the image show high tide or low tide? (Tide data for the Flamborough Head area can be found on the *Easytide*

website.) This image shows a time of day when the tide is neither fully in nor fully out. What do they think the place will look like at high tide and low tide? What will be covered or exposed? Explain that the area affected by the tide (the tidal zone) is visited by people for a variety of reasons and is also a habitat for plants and wildlife. What do people, especially children, enjoy doing on a seashore? What plants and wildlife live in or visit the tidal zone?

Main activity

- Children draw annotated sketches to show how the place will look at high and low tide. On both sketches, they label the physical features that can be seen in the image as well as the extent of the sea. What might be revealed when the tide is fully out? (Small sandy beach beyond the wave-cut platform, area of shingle, rock pools, etc.) They should include people or wildlife that might visit at low tide. What might people do in a place like this? (Crab-hunting in rock pools, fishing, walking a dog.) What wildlife might be seen?
- Children work on the sketches, either drawing them from scratch or using the outline (see **Activity sheet 1**). Prompt them to think about (and include in their sketches) the effects of waves hitting the cliffs at high tide and a range of features (physical, natural and human) revealed at low tide. They should label all the features clearly.

Plenary

- Ask the children to share their sketches and describe the features that they have included, particularly in the low tide sketches.

Differentiation (including use of LSA if available)

Depending on their abilities as writers or sketchers, encourage children to record their ideas appropriately using text and/or lines, shading, colouring, etc. An alternative way of carrying out the activity would be to use ICT. See the CD-Rom for ideas on this.

Resources

The key resource needed for the lesson is the image of part of the coast at Flamborough Head in North Yorkshire, which is included on the CD-Rom.

Easytide website (**http://easytide.ukho.gov.uk**).